Common Threads Playwork Classics Series

Adventure in Play

John Barron Mays

Second Edition

www.commonthreads.org.uk

ISBN: 978-1-904-79230-7

COMMON THREADS PLAYWORK CLASSICS SERIES
Series Editor: Shelly Newstead

Adventure in Play Second Edition

© John Barron Mays 1957

First Edition published 1957 by Liverpool Council of Social Service.

The right of John Barron Mays to be identified as the author of this Work has been asserted by him in accordance with sections 77 and 78 of the Copyright, Designs and Patents Act 1988.

Cover image © Angela Mays

All efforts have been made to trace the copyright holders for this work. In the event of any queries, please contact the publishers as below.

This document is an original document and reflects the legislation and policy of its time. It should not be used as a guide to current legislation or policy. Up-to-date information should be sought regarding current legal and good practice requirements.

Printed in the UK by Lightning Source UK Ltd.

All rights reserved. No part of this publication may be produced in any form or by any means, without prior permission of the publisher.

British Library Cataloguing in Publication Data
A catalogue record for this book is available from the British Library.

Common Threads Publications Ltd
Wessex House
Upper Market Street
Eastleigh, Hampshire
SO50 9FD UK
E: info@commonthreads.org.uk
W: www.commonthreads.org.uk

Registered Company Number 4500413.

Acknowledgements

'*Adventure in Play*' is the first of the Common Threads Playwork Classics Series, and, as with all new playwork initiatives, there has been a lot to learn. Sincere thanks are particularly due to Mrs Angela Mays and Professor Nicholas Mays for their patience and continued support for this experiment, and to Neil Bertram who made the whole project possible.

We are also very grateful to LCVS (Liverpool Charity and Voluntary Services) for supporting the re-publication of *Adventure in Play*.

Foreword
Tony Okotie, Chief Executive, LCVS
www.lcvs.org.uk

LCVS (Liverpool Charity and Voluntary Services) was established in 1909 and works with diverse communities across the city to make a positive difference to people's lives. We bring people and organisations together for positive change in communities through voluntary action and charitable giving.

Back in 1957, when we were Liverpool Council for Social Service, our predecessors had the pleasure to publish the first edition of *Adventure in Play* by John Barron Mays. Therefore we are delighted to see *Adventure in Play* back in print and it's quite timely as LCVS is currently running a programme in Liverpool to support and develop children's play.

Positive about Play is an exciting programme which engages with children and families during the school holidays at a time when many struggle for support. It helps ensure that every child in Liverpool has the same chance to succeed, even during holiday periods. Over the last two years, LCVS has led and worked with partners through the Play Partnership to develop *Positive about Play*, which has had fantastic results for children in the city.

With over 70 play organisations involved, support from Public Health, Liverpool Clinical Commissioning Group, The Mayor, elected members, and other trusts and donors, *Positive About Play* aims to not only provide free play activities but also to provide a range of additional services to support families. This includes a healthy eating programme, access to debt advice and training for play staff in supporting the Early Help Assessment Tool that means families in need are able to get the support they need, when they need it.

Adventure in Play pointed the way forward for many people who have worked in or championed children's play over the years and we are pleased to be able to support its re-publication nearly 60 years on.

II

Introduction

Nowadays the term 'adventure playground' is used to describe a wide range of playground provision for children, from small areas of commercially produced play equipment in pub gardens to large structures built from natural materials in woodland parks. However the original adventure playgrounds were created in the UK just after the Second World War, following a model invented by the Danish landscape architect Carl Theodore Sørenson, who had invented the Danish word 'Skrammellegeplads' to describe his idea of a boundaried space designated specifically for children within an otherwise adult-designed and dominated urban society (Andersson and Høyer, 2001, p.18). Whilst the precise origin of the term adventure playground is unclear (The Times, 1959; Allen and Nicholson, 1975, p.233), it became widely adopted after Lady Allen of Hurtwood used it in a leaflet published by the National Playing Fields Association (now Fields in Trust) in 1953 (Allen and Nicholson, 1975, p.233).

Adventure in Play was one of the first publications in English on these innovative and unorthodox spaces for children. Published by Liverpool Council for Social Service in 1957, its author, John Barron Mays, was at the time Warden of the Liverpool University Settlement, and he wrote this report as Chairman of the Pitt Street Juvenile Committee which oversaw the day-to-day operation of the Rathbone Street adventure playground. At the time of writing *Adventure in Play*, Mays was already developing his academic career. Two years previously, he had published a much more widely known and critically acclaimed work, *Growing Up in the City* (1955), which was ground-breaking in its approach to the 'problem' of young people in society, and influenced sociological theory and research for many years to come (Downes, 1989). Mays went on to write many other authoritative texts on the same theme, and later become the Eleanor Rathbone Professor of Sociology at Liverpool University (Lowson, 2015).

As Warden of the University Settlement, Mays' 'hands-on'

playwork experience would have been extremely limited. However he was very much a 'hands on' sociologist, in touch with the young people who occupied a great deal of his working life (see Mays, 1959), and his insight into the day-to-day running of the adventure playground clearly qualifies him as one of the adventure playground pioneers. *Adventure in Play* provides, as Hodges observed, a "penetrating appraisal of the experiment" (p.4) of Rathbone Street, detailing many of the practical challenges and pitfalls of running an adventure playground. With barely any literature to support the development of new projects, the adventure playground pioneers had to discover the best way of setting up and running these novel spaces for children from scratch (see Allen, 1953). Rathbone Street was part of a research project funded by the National Playing Fields Association "so that an assessment might be made of the value of this type of playground" (NPFA, 1960, p.3). Mays uses the term "operational research" to describe the process of 'learning through doing' adopted by the adventure playground pioneers, who learnt how to run adventure playgrounds by running adventure playgrounds (see Gutkind, 1952; Cambridge Children's Playground Association, 1957; Benjamin, 1958).

A vital part of the adventure playground experiment was learning from mistakes, an approach later summed up by Lady Allen of Hurtwood (Allen and Nicholson, 1975, p.249) as "If it works – splendid. If it fails, scrap it and try something else." With limited funding to try out this new and largely untested idea, the adventure playground pioneers were keen to find out as much as possible about what they regarded as a potential solution to one of the fundamental problems in society, which was succinctly summed up by Mays (p.5) as "the wide cleavage between youth and age, childhood and maturity". Children and adults were regarded as being fundamentally different in their nature, as Mays (pp.5-6) describes:

> "Children like disorder or find some invisible order therein. Most adults hate it. Children do not in the least mind being dirty. Most adults abhor it.

> *Children will find a source of enjoyment in the oddest and most unlikely play material: tin cans, milk bottle tops, broken slates, soil, cinders, firewood. The adult mind thinks of these things in terms of refuse and rubbish, and years for factory-made toys, areas of level tarmac, swings and roundabouts."*

The adventure playground pioneers believed that this fundamental difference in the natures of children and adults gave rise to differing and conflicting perspectives, as illustrated by Mays (pp.26-27):

> *"Many people who visited the playground found that their orderly and fastidious middle-class minds were horrified by the depressing appearance of the place. But the two little boys from dockland who "played the entire afternoon on the remains of the van, taking bits off one part and putting them in a different place" and the group of toddlers who spent "the entire day raking a mound of dirt together, transporting it to another spot, re-raking it and returning it to its original position" have a different and equally valid viewpoint."*

The clash of the dominant adult worldview and the contradictory view from childhood created a vicious cycle of rebellion by children and futile retaliation by adults. For the adventure playground pioneers it was simply a matter of fairness that children should have some time and space where, as Abernethy (1968, p.17) later put it, they could "do what they need to do and not what adults think they ought to do". Adventure playgrounds appeared to provide a temporary solution to this self-perpetuating war of the generations, and so the adventure playground pioneers set about finding out as much as possible about how to create spaces in which the business of childhood was prioritised. *Adventure in Play* was written in the hope that it would "stir public imagination and stimulate community action" (p.30) to develop adventure playgrounds which might serve the distinct needs of children by learning from the Rathbone Street experience.

The first publication of *Adventure in Play* was a significant milestone in the development of adventure playgrounds and the modern-day playwork profession. As the playwork profession has evolved from its adventure playground roots, it has generally failed to consider the lessons of its past (Cranwell, 1999; Conway, 2003, p.104). It is therefore hoped that this re-publication of *Adventure in Play* might stimulate new interest in what might be learnt from the original experiment of adventure playgrounds. Many of the challenges identified by Mays will still be very familiar to today's adventure playground workers, such as the recruitment and training of what Bengtsson (1970, p.174) later referred to as "the right sort" of adult, how to make the best of inadequate sites and finding sufficient resources to sustain children's interest on a limited budget. Mays' lifelong interest in trying to understand children's experiences from the perspectives of children themselves is reflected throughout the early adventure playground literature, a perspective which is often lost in modern-day playwork. *Adventure in Play* also raises several pertinent and much broader questions about the nature and purpose of the adventure playground experiment. Perhaps pre-empting adverse reactions to his 'warts and all' approach, Mays (p.26) stresses the importance of taking an experimental approach to the unknown quantity of adventure playgrounds:

> "The essence of an experiment is that it is experimental. A great many people forget this when they are looking round for what they like to call results. By results they mean things going in the way they think they ought to go. They cannot understand that positive results sometimes reveal themselves negatively, and that what does not take place can be as significant as what does."

Fifteen years and a few hundred adventure playgrounds later, Leo Jago (1972, p.8), then a Field Officer with London Adventure Playground Association, wrote

"Adventure playgrounds in London have grown out of the pioneer stage, they are not new babies to be gazed at in awe and wonder how the experiment will work out. They have reached adolescence and must choose their adult role." Perhaps one of the questions that might usefully be considered on reading *Adventure in Play* some sixty years from first publication is whether adventure playgrounds – and the playwork field they produced – have truly learnt from the adventure playground experiment, or whether there is yet more to be discovered.

Shelly Newstead

References

Abernethy, W. D. (1968). *Playleadership*. London: National Playing Fields Association.

Allen, Lady Allen of Hurtwood. (1953). *Proposed Organisation for Initiating Adventure Playgrounds*.

Allen, M. and Nicholson, M. (1975). *Lady Allen of Hurtwood: Memoirs of an Uneducated Lady*. London: Thames and Hudson.

Andersson, S.-I. and Høyer, S. (2001). *C. Th. Sørensen: landscape modernist*. Copenhagen: Danish Architectural Press.

Bengtsson, A. (1970). *Environmental planning for children's play*. New York: Praeger.

Benjamin, J. (1958). 'Adventure Playground Pioneer Social Experiment in Grimsby'. *Nursing Mirror and Midwives Journal*, 2nd May 1958.

Cambridge Children's Playground Association (1957). *Newmarket Road Adventure Playground - Holiday Experiment - A Report*.

Conway, M. (2003). 'Professional Playwork Practice'. In F. Brown (Ed.), *Playwork - Theory and Practice* (pp.101-113). Maidenhead: Open University Press.

Cranwell, K. (1999). 'The Role of the Study of History in the Playwork Profession', *PlayEd 1999A - Theoretical Playwork and the Research Agenda conference*. Ely: PlayEducation.

Downes, D. M. (1989). *Crime and the city: essays in memory of John Barron Mays*. Basingstoke: Macmillan.

Gutkind, P. C. W. (1952). *Report to Clydesdale Road Playground Committee - May 1952*.

Jago, L. (1972). *Draft Report*. London Adventure Playground Association.

Lowson, D. (2015). 'John Barron Mays (1914-87)'. *Journal of Playwork Practice*, 2 (1), pp.93-95.

Mays, J. B. (1955). *Growing up in the City*. Liverpool: Liverpool University Press.

Mays, J. B. (1959). *On the Threshold of Delinquency*. Liverpool: Liverpool University Press.

NPFA National Playing Fields Association (1960). *Adventure Playgrounds - a progress report*. London: NPFA National Playing Fields Association.

The Times. (Wednesday April 15th, 1959). 'Obituary - Sir George Pepler'. *The Times*, p.15.

ADVENTURE IN PLAY

The Story of the Rathbone Street Adventure Playground

by
JOHN BARRON MAYS
WARDEN OF THE LIVERPOOL UNIVERSITY SETTLEMENT

"The art of city planning is four-dimensional, consisting of length, breadth, height and imagination."

—HENRY S. CHURCHILL.

PREFACE

by

SIR REX HODGES, J.P.

Chairman of the Liverpool Council of Social Service

THE author of this moving study is himself the Chairman of the Pitt Street Juvenile Committee which was the body responsible for the day to day running of the playground experiment that is described. He is, therefore, somewhat in the position of a parent called upon to make a critical appraisal of one of his own children. Parents so placed generally fall over backwards in their efforts to avoid claiming too much for their progeny and in my view this appraisal by Mr. Mays definitely errs on the side of modesty.

It is right that the difficulties and shortcomings of the playground should be revealed in detail because knowledge of them will be invaluable to other organisers of playgrounds but it would be wrong to overlook the thousands of hours of happiness it has provided.

The two years of experiment that are described could not, of course, be honestly written up as a complete success story. There have been a good many weaknesses and errors large and small. The greatest shortcoming has been a lack of planning, but it is difficult to plan effectively when, first, you do not know exactly what it is you are planning, and secondly, you do not know what funds are going to be available. The site of the playground itself is a blitzed site and not a permanent open space and the lease of it is renewable only from month to month. This in itself has precluded long term planning and has necessarily restricted capital expenditure on the layout to a minimum.

It would be easy to evade an evaluation of the experiment by an argument to the effect that its results will be complete only when the children who have used the playground are themselves the parents of another generation of children and that even then the results will defy measurement. There is, however, a less complicated approach and Mr. Mays has indicated it by his claim that the experiment must be judged both as a piece of social service for the direct benefit of the neighbourhood and as a piece of operational research.

The measure of its success as a piece of social service is that the Liverpool Education Committee has agreed to continue the grant that was paid for an initial period of two years by the National Playing

Fields Association. So the playground has a future, and I think the difficult problem of its leadership may now be solved. Mr. Mays has indicated that the play leader is inevitably under-employed during the winter months and is needed to work impossible hours during the summer. An arrangement has now been reached whereby a male leader is employed jointly by the Pitt Street Committee and a nearby Mission in which he will be mainly responsible for the youth work. The economy thus achieved will enable the Committee to provide the necessary reliefs during the summer season, and to maintain the playground largely on a caretaker basis during the worst of the weather.

The measure of its success as a piece of operational research is that it has induced my Council to set aside some thousands of pounds to employ a playgrounds organiser and three play leaders for a further period of years on the understanding that the Liverpool City Council will, through its Parks and Gardens Committee, lay out and maintain playgrounds on the Swedish pattern.

It is important to draw a distinction between the "junk" playground that Mr. Mays has described and the "adventure" playground as provided in Stockholm and elsewhere. The latter is carefully planned in sections catering for sand and water play, constructional play, swings and roundabouts and junk, and may also include an area for ball games. An extensive "junk" playground almost inevitably becomes a waste of junk and thereby renders all the more difficult the task of shaping play into a creative thing. We believe that the adventure playground, which has a basic order for all its freedom and the element of choice which it clearly offers, will provide an environmental discipline and make the task of the play leaders, which is essentially that of leading play into constructive channels, very much easier.

My Council is much indebted to Mr. Mays and the Pitt Street Juvenile Committee and to the playleaders and others who have helped them. We feel that their struggle against odds has been infinitely worthwhile and has provided much happiness for the children and very valuable lessons for us. I am particularly glad that this careful and penetrating appraisal of the experiment has been written and I commend it to all whose imagination is stirred by the immense possibilities of such playgrounds.

Rex Hodges.

ADVENTURE IN PLAY

The Vision

FROM the window of my room in the University I used to be able to see beyond the high back-garden wall a typical small builder's yard. It was stacked with ladders of all lengths, planks, barrels, packing cases, house bricks, sacks of cement and plaster, wheelbarrows, buckets, spades, saws, tools of many fascinating shapes and varieties. There was also a battered van and a truck which would be a joy to drive along Hebridean roadways, and something which looked like —but couldn't possibly be—a portion of a spiral staircase. The whole place, were it not for the high protecting wall and the double-barred gate, was a children's dream of heaven! There were hundreds of dark and dusty places to explore; there were innumerable possibilities in the way of quickly erected hidey-holes; those pieces of timber would make a stockade for Long John Silver; that little platform was simply crying out for a Superman take-off. Any child with any imagination and any fund of "comic" lore in his memory could improvise endless happy hours in such a place. And once he had exhausted the furthest flights of imaginative invention he might like to return to earth by way of trying his hand at brick-laying or in sawing up wood to make a house for his pigeons. In any case he would be happy, mind and body creatively occupied, at peace with himself and with society, safe from the grosser dangers of road traffic and less inclined to want to break into a warehouse or swing precariously on the rear of laden wagons coming up from the docks. A scratch with a chisel, a bruise in falling, a grazed elbow, a hammered thumb—all amenable to the touch of iodine and the plaster bandage—are a small price to pay for such exhilarations, such voyages and destinations through a world of healthy dreams. Of such is the vision of an Adventure Playground, hybrid of the strip-cartoon and the junk yard.

In this country adventure, junk or constructional playgrounds— call them what you will! are still looked at askance. They are more than uncommon. They exist merely on the lunatic fringe of orthodox recreation. Resistance against them is widespread and even some educationists, administrators and social workers who, theoretically at least, know what their purpose is, are still appalled by the inevitable confusion, mess and dirt which they entail. All this is due to the wide cleavage between youth and age, childhood and maturity in our culture. Children like disorder or find some invisible order therein. Most adults hate it. Children do not in the least mind being dirty. Most adults abhor it. Children will find a source of enjoyment in the oddest and most unlikely play material: tin cans, milk bottle tops, broken slates, soil, cinders, firewood. The adult mind thinks of these things in terms of refuse and rubbish, and yearns for factory-made toys, areas of level tarmac, swings and roundabouts. Not that there is anything wrong in providing children with swings and roundabouts and see-saws, the despised "ironmongery" which is such anathema to the avant-garde. Adventure play is not to be thought of as a substitute for more orthodox types of playgrounds but as a supplement, a means of supplying the lost vitamins to the children's impaired recreational diet. Swings and roundabouts are part of the regular provision and are perennially popular but they do not meet all a child's needs. If anyone wants proof of this assertion let him unload a quantity of sand in one of the streets in the central area of any great city and watch the results. Instantaneously, as if called up by enchantment, children appear from all quarters, many equipped with bucket or wooden spade, to romp and revel in this most beloved of all play materials. Tenaciously they cling to every golden particle, scratching and flinging it about, letting it run through their fingers like dry fire, pushing it, prodding it, shaping it until all at last is swept away along gutters and drains.

Sand is a prerequisite of any type of adventure play as far as the younger children are concerned and in some way or another must be incorporated in any worthwhile playground. It is, of course, dirty and it treads into the house. After a while it gets full of "fleas". So local fathers and mothers complain but they can hardly believe that the fleas arrive as a result of spontaneous generation!

The ideas behind the adventure playground movement are, as one writer has so well said, "as old as history, as fundamental as childhood itself".[1] To build, to construct, to improvise, to put up and pull down are primitive activities which appeal to any normal child. "It is only when these natural inclinations are thwarted by an industrialised civilisation that adults have to think up alternatives"[2] and to recreate the conditions which make this sort of creativity possible. The urban child is cut off from all natural life, from growth of plant and tree, from water, stream or river, from sand on the seashore. Not surprisingly when he does get into the country he thinks of birds as targets for catapults and trees as things to be hacked down for firewood. If he finds crabs in a rockpool it will not be long before he is stoning them to death. The urban child is psychologically disorientated, cut off from man's natural roots, seldom called upon to battle with the elements or to learn to co-operate with nature. This

---

[1] "Adventure Playgrounds in Britain" in *Playing Fields*, April-June, 1955, p. 15.
[2] Ibid

is a deep sickness which no playground movement can as yet hope to cure. But it can make a beginning and the beginning is to teach and assist the child to use his hands and imagination in coping with whatever simple materials he finds, to allow him the satisfaction of putting one stone upon another, of placing a few planks together to form a hut, of digging a hole or lighting a fire in the open air. In some places re-education can go one stage further, encouraging contact with living, growing things by establishing a garden which the children can help to plan and where they can experience the great satisfaction of planting a seedling and watching it grow and come into flower.

If such a playground is to do its work properly it will require skilled and devoted leadership. Unfortunately few people are willing to try such work. There is no established profession of "playground leaders". There are no training courses. In fact little is known in this country beyond the few simple psychological principles that children like to play and that they often like to play messily and to make things. In order to discover more about the principles, the strong and weak points in this kind of play, the quality of leadership required and the sorts of activity most popular a number of experiments have been launched in recent years in various parts of the country. One centred on Liverpool had both local and national backing and its history and fortunes form the substance of this report. It is by no means typical but the story of its trials and triumphs and above all the possibilities for future development that it opened up will be of interest to people who contemplate similar projects elsewhere, its failures no less than its successes.

The Site

Liverpool's Adventure Playground was not an entirely new undertaking but was a new section grafted on to an already existing playground area. It is situated some half mile from the river front in a semi-residential, semi-commercial zone immediately adjacent to the city's commercial hub and lying close to the line of the central and southern docks. The area has a long history of social and economic disadvantage and has, in the past, been characterised by overcrowding, poor housing conditions, poverty and inferior educational opportunity. An extensive rehousing and redevelopment scheme has been undertaken since the end of the war and a great many blocks of corporation flats have been erected in place of the older insanitary property. There are, however, few open spaces available for children to play in safety and the nearest park is a bus ride away. As a consequence the streets are the traditional places where the children kick a ball, climb lamp-posts or build their brickbat houses and for this, if for no other reason, the provision of a comparatively spacious area for the recreation of the children of the neighbourhood was a prime necessity. The story of Rathbone Street Playground goes back to the year 1949 when a handful of social workers came together in the office of the University Settlement to see what they could do to help the children of the district and in particular to reduce the incidence of juvenile delinquency and misbehaviour generally. They began a long series of negotiations with the local authority which culminated in two pieces of derelict land, some 1,800 square yards in all, being leased to the Local Education Committee on their behalf. On this space a small football pitch with tubular steel goals was laid out while a slide, two swings, a roundabout and see-saw were provided for younger children. The cost of these fittings was entirely borne out of funds privately subscribed to the Committee. Shortly after a lifeboat was donated by a large shipping company, and this was set into the ground in concrete, filled with sand and used as a pen for toddlers.

The equipment was merely left there for the children to play with and the football pitch made available for any group of boys who wanted a game. At that time the committee had no idea of ever employing a full-time worker and they had expected to be able to run the playground with the help of the adults of the neighbourhood. One of the lessons they quickly came to learn was that many of the local people were entirely indifferent to the efforts being made on behalf of their children; some were obstructive, many were critical. Only a loyal and faithful handful, most of whom lived in Washington Street immediately adjoining the site, took an active interest in what was going on and volunteered to help. The staunch support of these Washington Street folk cannot be over-estimated. From the day the playground was officially opened by the Earl of Derby in the presence of literally hundreds of people in the midsummer of 1953 their helpfulness has been sustained without interruption. During those first fine nights gangs of marauding youths appeared from other parts of the city, roused by newspaper reports and bent upon sabotage. A handful of Washington Street people stood guard over the new equipment until one o'clock in the morning, waiting for the saboteurs to depart before going to their beds. They brought out their suppers and ate them sitting in the boat to the musical accompaniment of a guitar. One man stayed up so late at his self-appointed task that he overslept the next morning and lost half a day's pay.

Two retired Washington Street men have throughout the playground's history acted as honorary caretakers, filling gaps when the leaders have been absent, mending broken fences, oiling and repairing equipment, showing the lads how to use tools and generally being invaluable custodians of law and order. It is no exaggeration to say that without the support of all these families from Washington Street the playground would never have survived its early stages. Their support and loyalty is an example and a contrast to the indifference

Sand, most beloved of all play materials (p. 3)

Our first Lifeboat, "The Washington Queen" (p. 8)

Learning to use their hands (p. 5)

Building a Wall (p. 5)

Barrel-Trundling (p. 15)

Conveyor Belts as a Model Railway (p. 16)

Old Vans and Motor Cars (p. 17)

Old Tramway Sleepers as a Log Cabin (p. 17)

of the neighbourhood as a whole. One cannot help fearing that they belong to a vanishing generation and are survivors of a more responsible way of life than the post-war community is ever likely to create.

From very early days the local committee had the full support of the Council of Social Service through its Youth Organisations Committee. The idea of blitz-site playgrounds caught on and many such groups of local social workers came together with similar objects in view. Most of these Area Youth Welfare Associations, as they came to be called, were instituted by the city's Juvenile Delinquency Committee and given vigorous support by the Director of Education. But the Pitt Street Committee preceded all these other movements and associations and undoubtedly gave a direct stimulus to the growth of the type of work in the city as a whole. By 1953 Liverpool was extremely playground conscious. A committee of the Youth Organisations Committee kept a friendly and helpful eye on all developments and provided a substantial proportion of the necessary finance. A very valuable collaboration existed between the various members of the Y.O.C. committee, the central Juvenile Delinquency Committee, the Local Education Authority and the various local committees concerned with the day to day running of playgrounds in several parts of the city. The Youth Organisations Committee were keen to launch an experiment in constructional or adventure play and largely through their efforts the interest of the National Playing Fields Association was aroused and a grant of £800 offered for a two-year experimental period if such a playground could be launched in Liverpool.

The Pitt Street committee were asked to extend their boundaries incorporating a further 1,600 square yards of land, for an Adventure play area. They agreed. The necessary authority was obtained from the Corporation and in the early summer of 1954 the project began to take shape. A full-time woman leader was appointed and among her first jobs were the securing of equipment and materials and the supervision of the construction of a 6-foot chain link fence around the part of the site especially designated to adventure play.[1] The leader began amid a host of disadvantages, with nothing more than a stony and deserted space to commence adventure play. The fence was gradually constructed round her and odd pieces of equipment began to gather inside the crude compound, objects of lively interest to the children and of amazement to many passers by.

The site had much to recommend it. It offered plenty of space and was well clear of main road traffic. Moreover, it was already established as a play area and as such was well known to the local children and residents. A feeling of ownership and responsibility had already

[1] Experience showed that this fencing would not stand up to continued hard buffeting from rolling tyres, barrels, etc. The fence would have been much more satisfactory had the wire mesh been erected on top of a low stone wall. This would, however, have increased our financial outlay which at the time had to be kept to a bare minimum.

been created in the minds of most Washington Street families as was instanced by those who, during the early days when gangs of youths intent on destruction had arrived from other parts of the city, had conscientiously patrolled the area and thus protected the new equipment from serious damage. It lay, moreover, on land that was scheduled for redevelopment within the cathedral precinct, directly behind St. James Road and in full view of visitors leaving by the great west porch. Here transatlantic travellers come with their cameras to snap the local children playing in the shadow of the massive central tower and here, too, a few of the more enterprising youngsters indulge in brazen begging.

The surface of the playground formed its major drawback, since it covered what had once been rows of houses and stables and had no depth of soil at all. The ground, an amalgam of brick dust, broken glass and rubble had been covered with loose clinker. On dry days when the wind blew clouds of dust into eyes and throats it was an unpleasant place indeed. The football pitch had to be surfaced with soil and rolled before it was safe to play there but even this gradually wore away and was swept up in billowing clouds that rolled between the houses and down the street in an unending storm of dust. The surface in wet weather formed thick muddy pools which refused to evaporate and one of the earliest jobs performed by the children was the cutting of little channels and runnels down which the stagnant rain water could run off into the street drains. A further source of trouble arose from the fact that odd-jobbers and small builders had got into the habit of tipping their rubbish on the waste ground alongside the playground and this refuse in addition to the innumerable stones that were constantly being dug up from the ground, gave the whole site a brickfield appearance. Brickbats were a danger to life and limb. Antisocial groups would stand on the hillside sending fusillade after fusillade into the compound below. Cuts and bruises, the result of miscellaneous stone-throwings, were a regular part of the price paid for each day's ration of play. It became a routine job for the co-operative children to collect all unwanted stones and rubble into a heap so that friendly stone-crushers could come and take them away. Even so the quantity did not seem to dwindle. More bricks were excavated from the covered cellars of bombed houses and once again a stony tide swept across the never very orderly site to the dismay of all adults and the confusion of the harassed Play Leader.

The Sinews of Adventure Play

From the midsummer of 1954 the battle was on in earnest. Come dust, come brickbats, come gangs of obstreperous invaders, come saboteurs, thieving scrap-metal merchants and the I.R.A. itself the experiment went forward. One of its worst enemies and one against which there was neither protection nor redress was the weather. The summer of 1954 was particularly cold, wet and sunless and could hardly have been less favourable to the project.

The leader and committee seriously set about the task of acquiring materials for the type of constructive and creative play they were aiming to stimulate. Visits were made to builders' yards, workshops and factories. Letters were written to a great many firms and corporation departments in an endeavour to acquaint people with the playground's needs. In particular they had to convince contractors and other key folk that what might seem to them the merest scrap could be the very sort of equipment needed for adventure play. In the end a fair quantity of stuff was obtained and carted to the site where it was instantly put into use. Generally such scrap materials have a very short life. Amongst the expendables were reckoned all sorts of wood, logs, planks, off-cuts and barrels. Old rubber tyres were useful in building pliable forts but when the boys started rolling them about and crashing them into the fence they had to be removed. This was a great pity as they were popular and harmless to everything except the fence. But as this cost the committee £350 to erect the tyres had to be assembled and given back to their donors. Buckets, shovels, spades and rope all had a habit of disappearing as did the lovely little metal ladder. The neighbourhood was never very particular about where it obtained its firewood. One father sent his son up expressly to acquire a barrel which he wanted to paint and put in his own backyard. Keeping equipment was always a major problem and one that was only partially solved by erecting a small breezeblock hut during the second year. The metal drums and strips existed indefinitely even though twisted and bent out of all recognition. A load of soil which turned out to be largely composed of clay was purchased and dumped in the playground. It quickly set hard and was used as a scenic railway for barrel-trundling and, when this form of activity palled, the more adventurous boys got inside the barrels and rolled themselves down hill, ending up by crashing into the fence, which soon assumed a series of crazy bulges.

More permanent equipment which stood up to endless heavy wear and tear consisted of a large metal tank into which surplus bricks were always being thrown and which was constantly being used as a lavatory and having to be cleaned out, a furnace in which a real fire could be lighted and which had its own chimney to emit real smoke and a set of conveyor belts which were raised up on wooden blocks and lasted for many months as a sort of model railway for a diminutive metal car. A number of large sewer pipes were donated by the corporation and these were bedded down in concrete to prevent them moving and arranged in two groups. The children liked running in and out of them, trying to raise echoes with old tin cans. They were also very popular for chasing games like "cops and robbers" or "relievo" and could be used as a shelter on windy days. Short story readings were sometimes given in them when it was too wet to play outside but these had to be discontinued because more and more newcomers kept coming up and demanding an account of the preceding events. They also got very dirty and required regular hosing out. Like the large tank they were frequently made use of as lavatories. Since there were no lavatories on the site and no means of building them because of the expense and drainage, children either had to run off home or find a conveniently hidden corner. This lack of sanitation was a permanent handicap and it was as inconvenient for voluntary helpers and visitors as for the actual children.

There was also a whole series of old vans and motors which were immobilised and which the children invariably singled out for their most savage assaults, ripping off the roofs and tearing out the seating with the wildest of frenzies. A motor car or van to most of the children was an object of hate, a red rag to fire their aggression. They seemed to have little idea of looking after the structure so that it would remain as nearly like a real car as possible and so enhance the illusion. Not until the thing was reduced to the barest chassis was it left for the younger element to take possession of and utilise as an imaginary space ship or a racer screaming round hairpin bends.

A set of well-seasoned tramway sleepers proved to be a real investment. Too tough to hack into pieces, too heavy to remove altogether, they survived the roughest of games. A hole was dug in the ground and the sleepers placed around in the form of a stockade where many minic battles were waged. It was also used as a prison and by some malefactors as a safe spot for a sly game of cards and a gamble.

A second lifeboat was safely towed between the main gates and anchored in thick concrete. During the course of the next year a cabin with a small mast-pole was erected on its deck with a hole forward for a look-out.

One of the highlights of the first winter after a full-time leader took charge was the elaborate arrangements for November the Fifth. A tremendous pile of fuel was collected by the children, including old sofas and lounge suites and many off-cuts generously donated by a large firm of contractors. The two caretakers made a wooden arena with sleeper blocks around the stack and many children and their parents promised to come along after dark with their fireworks. Unfortunately the weather broke and the night turned out very wet. Undaunted the caretakers lit the fire, coaxed it into a roaring glow and so fiercely did it blaze that those who stood around it dried off more quickly than their clothes could absorb the wet so that they thought the rain had stopped. Children and parents came as promised and set off their squibs and crackers and rockets and catherine wheels. The great mound of timber burned long after the last explosion had echoed into silence and was still smouldering the following morning in spite of the long night's soaking.

During the first few months the playground, although acquiring a fair amount of "scrap" material, obtained little in the way of tools, partly because there was nowhere safe to store such things. But during 1955 a number of saws, hammers, mallets and paint brushes were bought and efforts made to get a more creative sort of activity going. The more dishonest boys hid tools so that they could later remove them to their homes. The leader chased one suspect to his own doorstep and demanded and obtained the return of the stolen property. But in spite of vigilance theft was rife and tools continued to disappear. The committee decided that the playground must have its own lock-up shed for storage purposes and began to raise money to that end. Meanwhile there were always the backyards of the good friends and neighbours of Washington Street to make use of for this as for many other purposes. Not only were their backyards used to store wood and paint but their cellars and kitchens were continually being invaded for water or being utilised as emergency dressing stations for the injured.

Efforts were made in the Easter vacation of 1955 to get everything going with a swing. The weather favoured this enterprise and children came flocking up in large numbers. A set of paving stones was moved and laid out inside the playground as a hopscotch pitch, numbers being painted by the boys on each separate slab. Soon paint and whitewash began to flow freely. Boys and girls and even some toddlers joined in the great crusade to create a brighter playground.

Typical entries from the log book at that time read:—

"A glorious day. Many children on the playground. Numbers easily reached 130 during the morning session. . . . Whitewashing operations commenced. The tunnel and all drain sections were done first and then all the concrete posts. . . . While this was going on another group painted the old van light grey. . . . Two other cars were painted, one green, the other yellow. Two eleven-year-old girls painted the green one. They were a bit shy at first but once they had started they set to and made a really good job of it. . . . The boat was finished and the name 'Pride of Rathy' painted on its side . . . a building competition in the afternoon. At 3.0 p.m. approximately two hundred children present. . . ."

These were the weeks when the playground was seen at its best. Numbers were large. There was much activity. In addition to the full-scale decoration scheme there were constant games of hopscotch and football in progress. Fires were lighted in safe places. The swings and merry-go-round were in perpetual motion. The football pitch was marked out—a gesture of supreme optimism. A sand-castle competition was staged for the tinies and about a dozen mothers came up to see what was happening and stayed to assist the leader.

The city Parks and Gardens Committee made arrangements for the delivery of a tremendous amount of brushwood which had a short-term yet very useful existence. The children dived in and out of the deep leaves and branches as into the sea. They stacked the pieces and arranged them to form wigwams in which they crouched and squatted as braves with their painted squaws. And when the brushwood tents collapsed and dried out a little they were always useful for kindling fires, with or without permission. On more than one occasion these inflammable branches had to be extinguished by buckets of water hastily carried from Washington Street backyards. Once the fire brigade was summoned, only to arrive after the blaze had been quelled.

Periods of depression, frustration and gloom were probably more frequent than these fleeting golden days of triumph. Log entries record some of the trials that met the leader as she faced each day afresh: —

"The cabin has been continually smashed and now we have no wood to repair it. . . . Two barrels are missing. . . . Arrived at the playground at 10.0 a.m. Rain was just starting and rapidly became worse. I found that the mast had been snapped off . . . scrap metal had been flung round the ground. . . . Once again the gang had been at work and the huts, etc. had again been wrecked . . . spent the main part of the day clearing up the mess. . . ."

However, despite the damage incurred after nightfall, the children still attended and seemed to derive satisfaction from their activities. On wet days they sometimes sheltered from the rain, huddled in one of the makeshift huts or packed into the draughty drain sections, and sang songs. There were occasional fights between rival gangs. Once a boy lost his temper and flung a brick which struck the leader on the jaw. On another occasion when teenagers refused to leave the precinct after nightfall one of the playground's intrepid custodians was not to be so easily put off. Linking a hose pipe to his bathroom tap he shot a jet of cold water out through his back window and sprayed the trespassers until they finally fled in confusion. The police at this time were very active and most co-operative. Special visits were made throughout the evening sessions and as a result a number of incidents were avoided and many anxieties were allayed.

Newspaper publicity in the early months drew a plague of spivs and scrap metal thieves to the playground. One man was discovered with a spanner quietly dismantling the carburettor from the shooting brake and preparing to make off with it. He admitted that he had read all about the playground in the *Echo*, spotted the very model of his own car in a photograph and having a damaged part to replace had travelled all the way from Hightown to collect a spare. On another occasion two brothers arrived with a handcart and proceeded to pile it up with bits of scrap metal. The leader protested and was insulted but gave such a full description that the two spivs were quickly apprehended by the police, brought to court and fined five pounds each—a very expensive way of collecting about a guinea's worth of old metal.

As the summer of 1955 wore on it was clear that the interest of the children was waning. Numbers fell off sharply and of those who came few wanted to do anything constructive. They either played ball games, messed about on "the ironmongery" or, on the really hot days, sunbathed and lazed around. A few brought food and had picnic teas and one little family camped out beneath two pieces of tin and an old shawl belonging to the baby.

In some ways it was fortunate and in other ways unfortunate that the adventure part of the playground had to exist alongside other and better established forms of play and to compete with slides and swings, etc., and the attractions of a ready-made football pitch. There must have been occasions when these counter-attractions stole the children's interest from the more arduous type of constructional play. Nevertheless it did mean that when children came into the adventure compound it was not merely because they had nothing else to do. They came from choice—and in these circumstances everything that the adventure section succeeded in accomplishing was done by virtue of its own intrinsic merits. It is clear that constructive play with scrap materials is not an alternative to be abandoned lightly but a genuine form of recreation existing in its own right.

It was obvious that the novelty was wearing off for many of the children who had originally flocked to the playground. They had been content for a while in using junk materials to construct huts, wigwams and underground dens as realistic stage properties for games of cowboys and indians or cops and robbers. The girls had derived pleasure from making little houses of loose stones, organising tea parties or in running little shops. Girls and boys of all ages up to fifteen had enjoyed the painting operations of the Easter vacation. The toddlers and tinies still attended in full force but the eleven plus children were rapidly losing interest. At this stage it was obvious that more skilled work was required to which the older boys and girls could apply their energies. The fierce competition of trips to New Brighton or to the parks or the fairground or the cinema was beginning to be felt. The moment had come when only an abundance of materials, particularly wood, together with the services of a skilled instructor and an adequate supply of tools might have revived the interest of the older children and brought the whole project back into energetic activity. But none of these requisites was available. Instead the leader was obliged to spend a great deal of time coping with the protection and construction of the new store hut and in arranging for the digging of the drains that were to be laid for the proposed drinking fountain. The breeze-block hut from which so much had been expected turned out to be another disappointment. Part of it fell or was knocked down during the building process and had to be re-erected. At a later date during the period while the second leader was off in hospital for a month the back wall of the hut was broken in and most of the equipment, wood, tools and paint were stolen. As a place for safe storage it was obviously not strong enough and as a retreat during inclement weather it was much too small. It had, however, one useful function. A tap and basin were installed for washing and drinking and after the drinking fountain had been irretrievably smashed the hut had to be used for this purpose. The story of the drinking fountain is one of repeated misfortune. Money became available for this necessary amenity but on account of involved negotiation with city authorities and later with plumbers it was installed just too late for the warm summer months. It was erected in the November of 1955 and within a week or so was destroyed. Once again the damage was wanton and carried out by unknown marauders in the night. Throughout the following summer the broken bits lay in the hut but the bills came punctually in each quarter from the corporation department which had to be paid. The whole project including laying drains and hiring a meter cost the general fund £125 and produced little in return.

And so amid disasters and disappointments the school holidays ended, the first experimental year ran out and some of the main purposes and objectives remained untested.

Unfortunately at this time the playground suffered a further disaster as a result of a change of leaders. The first leader, who had remained at her post for a period of some sixteen months, handed over the task to a very short-lived female successor who, during six months' official leadership, had several spells off work owing to ill-health. This change over of leaders during the vital middle stage of the project was a major disaster which unfortunately could not have been foreseen or prevented. Change of personnel is one of the risks that social service agencies are forced to run and one to which experimental pioneer projects are particularly prone.

Children's Attitudes

One of the factors which continually pulled against the work of the adventure playground was the lack of a tradition for creative play in the neighbourhood as a whole. Knocking things down, bashing, combat, aggression, destructiveness had a much firmer hold on the minds and imaginations of the children than the arduous toils of construction, creation, organisation, planning and design.

"In the afternoon," runs the log book for an October day, "after the usual game of rounders, I saw that some small girls of the six to ten age group had laid out the ground plan of a model house in bricks. Only two bricks high the interior was most carefully adorned with stone armchairs, beds, fireplaces, tables and so on, and had been decorated with clumps of grass (altogether a charming effort) but merely scorned by the boys who proceeded to do their best to wreck it."

The thirteen years and over boys were very conscious of themselves as "men". Football and cricket were male activities and therefore could be played in public without shame but to be seen playing an imaginative game, albeit an aggression-releasing activity, was thought of as childish or "cissy". An amusing entry in the log book illustrates this very point:

"A gang of boys inside the compound asked me to go away because they felt 'daft' if I watched them playing pirates. . . . I watched this game from the far side of the playground and it was highly entertaining to see some of these 13-14 year-olds being shot and dying among the brushwood."

Some of the boys also showed themselves to be more responsive to a man's approach than to a woman's. The playground's second leader commented: "It was amazing to see how the somewhat lazy boys immediately responded to Mr. Miller's suggestion of clearing bricks from the base of the fence. I could suggest this a hundred times and could only produce a very reluctant response. The suggestion coming from a man seems to be much more palatable."

But most of the girls welcomed the fact that the leader was a woman and found in her someone to talk to, to confide in and to share their own experiences of life with. They perhaps needed a companion rather than an adventure play leader and were more interested in personal relationships than in building or construction.

It is not easy, therefore, to generalise on the ages or sexes of the children who attended the playground, though it would seem that the purely adventure side of the playground on the whole appealed more to the boys than the girls. But there were a few who were very regular in all age groups and from both sexes. The toddlers were perhaps the most consistent attenders of all. The older boys and girls had phases of regularity broken by periods of boredom or absence in pursuit of other attractions. But most of them needed what was being offered to some degree and at some stage of their development. For the most part the playground relied upon a local catchment area of about a quarter of a mile on every side, but there were children who travelled further, some even arriving from the north end of the city. Attendances revealed a definable rhythm both in regard to the time of year and day. Late spring, cool summer days and early autumn were the best periods, school holidays at Easter being particularly well attended. Excessive cold or heat deterred most children. In midsummer they felt too tired or lazy to do anything but loll about while in the winter months, between October and March, their fingers were too stiff and their limbs too chilled to stand for very long in the open air. Not many children appeared at week-ends during the morning, because on Saturdays they were either doing messages or attending the morning film club show while on Sundays they were either at church or stayed longer in bed. Afternoons and evenings at week-ends showed the best attendances. A falling-off was noticeable at about 4.30 p.m. when they began to drift home for tea but numbers built up again during the lighter evenings between 7.0 p.m. and 9.0 p.m. It was remarkable how late some of the youngest children stayed. There were often well over a hundred in all three sections of the playground as late as 9.30 p.m.[1]

There were inevitably a great many accidents. So many children crowded together with so many opportunities for mutilating one another were bound to produce a steady flow of abrasions, cuts and bruises with the occasional more serious wound requiring stitching or a fractured bone. Statistically, however, the slide appeared to be the highest risk while the permanent ironwork equipment generally produced more accidents than the junk and scrap materials in the Adventure Playground proper. From the point of view of insurance against such accidents any local authorities contemplating the organisation of a similar playground in their own areas would find that a trifling addition to the amount covered by their existing playground accident policy would be adequate cover for any such development.

Discipline was always a problem but it would be misleading to suggest that the majority of children using the site were unruly. But there were always the small gangs or aggressive individuals who could upset the atmosphere, wreck other children's efforts at building, pour scorn on the orderly and even provoke fights.

It is impossible to estimate how far disciplinary troubles on the playground itself were a result of having a woman in charge or how far even the toughest boys' respect for feminity worked in the opposite direction. Certainly there was no particular kudos to be derived from "taking the micky" out of a mere girl. A male leader might have been considered a more worthy opponent to bait and badger.

Some of the more responsible parents felt that there ought to be better discipline and tighter control on the playground than there was. On the other hand, too strong measures would only drive away those very children the project was hoping to assist. Worse still it might turn boys who were merely being irritating into active enemies. It must be remembered that many of the problem children, being so

---

[1] As there was only one paid leader to cover these long hours, the voluntary assistance rendered by two or three of the local men was invaluable. In this way it was possible to arrange for the leader to have one full day's leave each week in addition to Saturday and Sunday mornings.

uncertain in their own minds about their own basic relationships and suspicious of any well-meaning adult, needed to test out their new leader's patience and endurance and discover how far her interest and affection were genuine and how far a mere matter of professional drill. This uncertainty produced much baiting of "Miss", casual stone-throwing, hiding of keys and other annoyances which could disrupt the proper purpose of the playground for hours. So, too, could clashes between rival gangs, each striving to drive the other away from the play area or competing for the proprietory interest and attention of the leader. There was also the usual clash between boys and girls ("Oh, Miss, Georgie won't give us a go on the swing an' 'e's spittin' at us!") and a small proportion of direct bullying. Part of the leader's daily work had to be devoted to straightening out these clashes and tensions, allaying anxieties and fears, before she could possibly hope to get a building competition going or ask for assistance in clearing up the site.

Committees

The Pitt Street Committee which managed, and at times mismanaged the playground's affairs was self-appointed and self-renewing body, consisting of school teachers, a church and social workers in the area, none of whom were truly indigenous. This absence of local folk on the committee was a real source of weakness which could not be overcome except by the device of constituting what we called a parents' committee drawn from a few selected families living in the immediate vicinity of the playground. It would have been better and more economical of time and energy to have appointed these parents to the governing body, but it was doubtful if local public opinion would have tolerated such a situation. The pattern of social service organisations was well understood in the neighbourhood: people, the rather posh middle class people, came in from outside and took over all the business of management. Local folk could of course help at the practical level, but not take the more vital decisions or appoint the workers. Any local people who might be able and willing to undertake such responsible work would be up against strong resentment from those less able or those who had not had the same opportunity to become bosses. The charge of "big-headedness" would be levelled against anyone who was willing to assume responsibility and even though that individual might be prepared to assert and accept his social differences it would have been a bad thing for the committee and the playground as a whole to have appeared to set up local distinctions or to choose between one person and another.

For these reasons the parents' committee were not given any executive power although, in fact, they exerted considerable influence. Nor was it formed at an early date. The adventure side of the experiment had been in existence for well over a year before the parents could be brought together. The children's own committee preceded it by nearly twelve months. This latter group was easily formed but much harder to retain in being. Children volunteered for the sheer novelty of taking part in something new, something which might prove exciting to bolster up their need to be important. They put forward plenty of ideas. One thing they requested was a badge of office which was discussed at great length. Among other duties, which naturally involved them all taking a responsible attitude while on the playground itself, some of the girls helped the leader to make her daily count of heads for noting up in the log book. They also tended minor cuts and bruises. The post of secretary was most difficult to fill, everyone appointed to that job proved very dilatory at writing up the minutes. The boys turned out to be less committee-conscious than the girls. They disliked being different and were reluctant to assert any sort of authority. Alec Beale came to the leader after the third time the committee had met and sadly offered his resignation. He felt he could not carry out his duties although he would have liked to have been able to stay on the committee. But his pals wouldn't support him and he couldn't go against them and so he had better give up the attempt.

Thus the children's committee in spite of the backing from the schools continued to fire on one cylinder for a long time, the boys failing to do their side of the work. When the second leader took up the task she endeavoured to form a new committee with four boys and four girls but found the going equally hard. The same pattern of interest and inertia appeared. Very soon the log book notes:

> "Had a meeting of the girls on the committee. The boys had come to the conclusion that they were not really interested enough in the playground to carry out the duties expected of them. The girls wrote a letter of thanks to Messrs. B—— for the gift of climbing equipment. They were all very sensible and produced a good letter with little help from me."

This failure of the boys to sustain a responsible interest in their own activities is probably closely connected with the general adult attitudes which characterise the neighbourhood as a whole. The fear of being thought different, of alienating oneself from the rest of the gang militates against any willingness to exert discipline against one's peers even in cases where it is felt that strong action should be taken. Alec Beale understood the dilemma in which he was placed and made his decision. Other boys manufactured excuses, e.g. that they hadn't any real interest in the playground anyway. Yet we know that it was the boys who mainly used the adventure section rather than the girls, although by the time they were thirteen or so they came to think of themselves as too grown up for such forms of play.

Both the children's and parents' committees were hand-selected. The adult group which was created by the second of the playground leaders showed itself to be a most valuable and helpful body once initial doubts had been dispelled. Its eight members were all close neighbours and lived in the same street immediately backing on the playground.

Merely going on to the ground and telling offenders to behave properly they felt to be ineffective. Only from the security of established authority demonstrated by some official symbol could they undertake the task.

The diffidence and doubt in the minds of many of the adult committee sprang from the rough-respectable dichotomy observable in all social relationships. There were the roughs who were no good, for whom it was not worth while doing anything, who would come and taunt you and spoil your effort and the respectable families who tried to keep themselves to themselves, to bring up their children to be clean and orderly and law-abiding. The adult committee was heavily weighted on the respectable side. This was only to be expected as they were the only source of leadership the district offered. Even they were dubious, hesitant and disillusioned. The leader had to bend all her efforts to making her committee realise their value, accept difficulties without withdrawal from the struggle and convince them that their help would be genuinely appreciated. She succeeded and the committee flourished. They commenced to make suggestions about improving the site and succeeded in putting the leader in touch with the manager of a firm they knew who donated a free load of sand. They helped to police the playground, putting out fires and preventing people walking away with wood or scrap. Two of them went out to obtain material themselves, calling at firms and begging several tins of paint for the children.

After every meeting a collection was made and ten shillings contributed to the playground fund. The children followed suit and collected pennies at each session which were kept in a match box and duly found their way into the general kitty. The resignation of the second play leader occasioned by ill-health brought this valuable work to a close. When the playground is again in the position to reopen with the services of a professional leader it will be a wise step to begin by reforming the parents' committee and attempting to make them full participants in any future development.

It would appear that there are a sufficient number of adults of the right calibre living close to the playground for it to become much more of a neighbourhood activity than it has yet been. The story of the guardianship of the equipment during the long summer nights of 1953, together with the happy experiences of the short-lived parents' committee, emerge among the more hopeful findings of what has from some aspects been an ill-starred venture.

The Institutional Framework

In establishing the adventure playground with its own full-time leader, committee and services, a new social institution had been injected into the structure of the neighbourhood and a fresh series of relationships thereby created. The leader was at the centre of a complicated network consisting of the schools, churches, youth clubs and the Settlement on one hand and the civic authorities and the Youth Organisations Committee on the other. There were further the individual families to take into account and the various cross-currents of jealousy, suspicion, pride and hostility that flowed between street and street, family and family, area and area.

The local schools, interpreted by the words of their head teachers, were friendly and welcoming. Two schools made substantial contributions and one headmaster who was on the local playground committee gave both leaders invaluable advice and comforting counsel. All three schools which were approached agreed to allow selected scholars to join the children's committee, and to attend meetings during school hours (usually at the Settlement or at St. Vincent's R.C. School), thus giving this aspect of the playground's work their moral and practical support.

The churches were equally amicable. One Anglican and one R.C. church were constantly represented on the management committee and, though there was little that either priests or parishioners could do beyond evidencing goodwill and attending meetings, this they did and in so doing allied themselves with the leader and helped to build up a united front in the neighbourhood.

Reference has already been made to the sympathetic co-operation received from the police, for whom the playground constituted in some of its aspects an extension of their worries rather than a relief from pressure. Through the work of the Juvenile Liaison Officer for "A" Division they were represented on the management committee and actively associated with the original inception of the Pitt Street committee and of the whole playground movement in the city.

The Settlement through its staff and residents gave much time and effort to the scheme, and was particularly valuable in offering both leader and committee a headquarters meeting place, a base for the conduct of operations, a storehouse and a refuge in wet weather.

The Windsor Boys' Club members spent several evenings clearing bricks from the site. They also made use of the football pitch for organised matches as did one of the local Play Centres. Local schools occasionally organised games there during school hours and one of the infants' departments frequently sent up a batch of children to enjoy a little controlled exercise in the morning sunshine.

Almost without exception local organisations and institutions welcomed the amenities of the playground and did what they could to assist in its work. Much greater use would have been made of it had the play space been bigger and cleaner. There can be no doubt whatsoever that the availability of such a playground could be a great boon to all schools and clubs in the district as well as a blessing to parents and children. A playground, properly laid out and supervised is, in fact, one of the absolutely necessary amenities for healthy urban living and something that, in this country at least, we have been lamentably slow to realise.

Leadership Rôles and Social Change

It is not intended that this brief report should develop into a sociological analysis yet something must be said of the motives and techniques employed during the project. The playground leader in her capacity of social worker attempting to bring about some sort of social change endeavoured to influence children and parents in a particular direction, leading them to the idea of a more constructive use of leisure and towards a more responsible attitude towards the problems of socially acceptable and unacceptable behaviour. Ideally her work would be on two distinct fronts, with the juveniles on the playground and with the adults in their homes. She would also operate at two levels, in two separate capacities. She would be at one time the playground "Miss" in charge of what the children invariably called "the Swings" and at another she would be the social worker at large, with a roving commission to do whatever job she found a matter of urgency. On the playground side she would be a group worker, spending most of her time with clusters of children with little time for individual attention, while, outside the playground she could undertake a limited amount of what we may call case work, trying, that is to say, to assist individuals or individual families to cope with their personal problems.

Such a job calls for an unusual combination of skills and an exceptional amount of physical and nervous energy. In fact neither of the two leaders succeeded at both levels. The first leader had her main success in the rôle of playground "Miss", collecting material, stimulating creative play, keeping law and order. The second leader's bent was in the opposite direction. Deeply interested in the individual, she found the actual daily grind on the playground an unbearable strain, but in her committee work and in contact with individual children or adults her sympathy and tact made her a most successful social catalyst, assisting people to sort out their problems and giving them insight into their own personalities and encouragement to find appropriate solutions. It was in some ways disastrous that the two successive leaders should have had such widely different approaches and talents for the job. Continuity of practical work was destroyed but, at the same time, their very differences contributed to the experiment and furthered knowledge.

What qualities and abilities should an adventure playground leader possess? Were sturdy commonsense, a natural physical robustness, ability to stimulate creative play, skill in making use of scrap material and a straight eye for a hammer and chisel of primary importance? Was the job best suited to one equipped with traditional group work techniques? Or were the hidden objectives more important? Was the quiet infiltration into the neighbourhood, building up confidence, developing a wide network of personal relationships with young and old more valuable? And valuable in what way? The former type of leader could achieve more tangible results in the way of cleverly constructed wigwams, space ships in old motor cars, stockades and hideyholes but how deep does such work go, how far does it really influence human behaviour, change attitudes, and, in this case, help to reduce delinquency? It is, of course, impossible to say which approach is ultimately the more important. On the basis of the Rathbone Street experiment one would be inclined to say that both approaches are equally valid and that neither is complete without the other. The techniques are not alternatives but complements of each other. The actual work done on the playground is justified by the enrichment it brings into the lives of children deprived of other outlets for their energies and impulses. By releasing imagination, by acquiring simple skills, by learning to use hand and eye constructively they will be the happier and the easier to control. But it should go a lot deeper than that. Through personal contact on the playground relationships between social worker and individual children can be developed which are strong enough and warm enough to assist the acquisition of new habits and attitudes in the place of older and less satisfactory behaviour. In this sense the work of the playground is a way in, a method of getting into contact with the children and the neighbourhood, a functional penetration, a banner and *raison d'être* which people can understand and appreciate. Without the day to day work on the actual playground the social worker would be rootless, hindered in establishing contacts and an object of deep suspicion.

Prevention of Delinquency

How much misbehaviour was obviated by the mere physical existence of the playground? How much crude energy was harmlessly expended which otherwise might have been directed against property and released in window-smashing or warehouse-breaking? The answers to these questions can only be guessed but never objectively measured. We can only assume that it did exert some kind of influence which may be termed social sublimation and in this way save the ratepayer

A second Lifeboat anchored in Concrete (p. 18)
"*The Pride of Rathy*"

A Hop-Scotch Pitch from Paving Stones (p. 20)

A Toddlers' Tea Party (p. 25)

Running their Own Shop (p. 26)

Huts and Dens (p. 25)

Encampment (p. 25)

Foundations for Log Cabin (p. 5)

Grouped Sewer Pipes (p. 16)

and the civic authorities a fair amount of time, effort and money. The report of the Liverpool City Lighting Engineer for the year 1954-55 estimated that it cost £4,200 to replace the street lamps wantonly destroyed by hooligans. It is in terms of such wholesale and widespread destruction that we must compute the possible value of playgrounds in the city centre and soberly estimate the possible dividend that may be earned by spending a little more money in preventing misbehaviour and perhaps less in unconstructively repairing its consequences.

The playground's second leader set herself the task of attempting the reformation of all trouble makers by concentrating on building up confidence, affection and mutual trust. The log book illustrates this attention given to the individual child in the setting of his own home:

> "I visited the mother of one of my boys who has been behaving particularly badly. We discussed the fact that he was going around once again with a boy much older than himself and whose influence was not the best. . . . I asked his mother to try for a time to ignore his actions or even better try to make him realise their foolishness rather than exaggerating the badness of them. . . ."

One boy at least found this type of approach based on personal relationship rather than upon threats of punishment almost too much to bear. Sometimes he followed the leader round like a pet dog, at other times he abused her, threw stones and swore at her. "Ah, Miss," he glumly lamented, "before you came 'ere all the kids used to take things from the trucks an' we used bad language, but you're trying to make everyone good 'ere. I think I'll start goin' down to the docks again."

A fair amount of time was expended trying to bring this particular young delinquent to consent to a change of behaviour and a realisation of the wrongness of his ways. He, like so many of his pals, had an irritating habit of retreating into the safety of the group just when he had been brought to the brink of making a major promise to reform. The leader had to battle constantly not only with the individual but with the group, dealing with the boy and his particular gang or set at one and the same time. Not all the children were unresponsive. There were signs that real co-operation in the deeper matter of delinquency-prevention had been achieved.

One bright Sunday morning in January two boys met the leader as she walked in the direction of the playground with the news that the wireless shop had been broken into and there was money laying in the cash-register waiting to be stolen. Somewhat agitated they conducted her to the place and begged her to do something. Evidently the presence of exposed money in such circumstances spelled danger for them. They wanted to be taken away from temptation and from the risk of any possible incrimination. They straightway conducted the leader to the nearest police station and had the matter officially reported. Having done what they considered their duty all returned to the playground to get on with the business of play.

On a further occasion a boy was recommended to join a nearby youth club in order to keep him away from dangerous companions. He did not turn up on the arranged night. Thereupon the leader called at his home, conducted him to the club and helped overcome his shyness by staying with him during the initiatory conversation while he received his new membership card.

In these and many other ways goodwill and interest were expressed so that the leader became a welcome visitor at many homes in the neighbourhood. Her visits were not always occasioned by the delinquency or misbehaviour of the children. Sickness and consultation on other matters brought her in close touch with the people she was striving to serve and every visit, every friendly contact, established the work of the playground more firmly in people's minds and extended its influence for good.

Assessment

The essence of an experiment is that it is experimental. A great many people forget this when looking round for what they like to call results. By results they mean things going in the way they think they ought to go. They cannot understand that positive results can sometimes reveal themselves negatively and that what does not take place can be just as significant as what does. Moreover, an experiment is conducted to see what will or will not happen. When it has told us this much it has fulfilled its objective.

Errors of this sort have led some critics and some idealists into a serious under-assessment of the value of the adventure playground. Because the playground was not always filled with eager, happy children rapturously engaged in building houses and making an intelligent use of the scrap materials available, they have been apt to write it off as a failure, forgetting that these very periods of inactivity are significant aspects of the project's experimental design.

Those who have been in close touch with the playground from its original conception to the present time are much less gloomy about its value either as a piece of operational research or as simply a piece of social service in its own right. A great many children have passed a great many happy hours at Rathbone Street during the past five years and it is in terms of such human happiness that any long term extension of its work must be evaluated. Impressions of outsiders and of adults are often misleading. Many people who visited the playground found that their orderly and fastidious middle-class minds were horrified by the depressing appearance of the place. But the two little boys from dockland who "played the entire afternoon on the remains of the van, taking bits off one part and putting them in a different place" and the group of toddlers who spent "the entire day raking a mound of dirt together, transporting it to another spot, re-raking it and returning it to its original position" have a different and equally valid viewpoint.

In spite of all its shortcomings, many of which were the result of hasty planning and lack of solid financial support, in spite of mistakes made by its management committee and the errors of its two appointed leaders, in spite of the roughness of the site, the endless brickbats, the noise, the dirt, the disorder, sufficient evidence has accrued to support the main thesis on which the playground was established—that given the tools, the materials, the adult interest, advice and support children will indulge in constructional play, they do derive satisfaction from using hand and eye in making and building, fetching, carrying, painting and digging. Where the playground failed was in the paucity of its provision, the meagreness of its equipment, its shortage of skilled instructors and almost total lack of storage space and security. These are things that in the future could be remedied. They are no more inevitable than the community allows them to be.

It is doubtful, however, if this type of play in this culture and in this climate is an all-the-year-round activity. There seem to be definite periods, between Easter and autumn when constructional play is popular. Further it appears, in this neighbourhood at least, to appeal more to boys than to girls and to the under-fourteen-year-old boys more than others. Toddlers, however, of both sexes seem to find perpetual delight in this sometimes rather messy sort of play.

Moreover, it has been proved that in Liverpool 1, there are sufficient local residents interested enough and capable of giving constructive help to a professional leader to justify the formation of a parents' committee. Such an adult committee is invaluable in so far as it is able to assume responsibility in the leader's absence for guarding both the equipment and the reputation of the playground.

Even though the girls do not on the whole enter completely into the building and digging activities offered them in the adventure section of the playground it is clear that they place a very high value on the opportunity of entering into close personal relationship with the play leader. They obviously need someone in whom to confide and with whom they could discuss their ideas and dreams about life. When the leader invited a party of the children over to her house for tea they reciprocated by inviting her to go out with them, one of the older girls acting as banker and collecting enough money from the others to pay for them all to go to the cinema. This sort of reciprocal relationship, although it has little to do with adventure playgrounds as such, turned out to be of great importance in the day-to-day organisation of the actual job. The girls especially lack feminine models with whom they can identify themselves and enjoy a safe and educative relationship, based on mutual respect and at the same time warmed by genuine two-way affection. In other words an adventure playground leader is also a human being and a social worker, compelled by conscience and sensitivity to others' needs to supply not only bricks and mortar, saws and hammers, wood and nails, but also those impalpable things, the emotional demands of children of all ages for security, companionship and love.

Recommendation

In the light of these last two years day-by-day experience in Rathbone Street there are several important findings which can now be placed before the sponsors of the original scheme in the form of recommendations. Enough has surely been said to show that the project succeeded both as an experiment, providing answers to certain questions, and as a job of work at the plain social work level.

Its rewards could be greater if sufficient support could be rallied to develop this type of work not only in Liverpool 1 but in other heavily built-up central areas of the city where the teeming, restless multitude of young children create by their very vitality a perpetual series of social problems.

1. *Leadership.* An adventure playground which aims to service up to one hundred and fifty children during a full session requires the services of more than one adult leader. One person is simply unable to cope with the spate of the demands made upon him at such times or to occupy usefully more than a handful of children.

Moreover, leadership of such a venture calls for such a rich and unusual combination of skills that it is unlikely that they will all be found in any one individual adult. Not only must the leader have deep understanding of and sympathy with children, be able to make good relationships with juveniles and adults alike but he or she must also be sufficiently knowledgeable in practical matters to be able to see the possibilities of scrap material, to understand simple manual skills and be able to administer rudimentary instruction. To these gifts must be added administrative ability, skill in handling committees, a talent for begging, a fluent tongue for making public speeches or appeals and the gift of literary composition for recording significant details and compiling reports.

A sensible arrangement would be the appointment of two joint-leaders, a man and a woman, chosen for the suitability of their personalities and the relevance of their acquired skills. A man, for example, to cope with the older boys, capable of giving simple instruction in handling tools and able to exert firm discipline when necessary and a woman to supply the individual touch, responsible for the case work side of the job and skilled in making creative human relationships, would make an excellent combination to undertake the complex work which had hitherto been the exclusive burden of one person.

2. *Seasonal Nature of the Work.* It seems clear that an adventure playground does not offer full-time occupation for the entire calendar year. The most active periods extend from the school holidays at Easter to the end of official summertime in October, a span of a little over six months. During the winter, out-of-door work is made extremely difficult by short days and bad weather, and can only be pursued at week-ends and for a few days during the Christmas break.

In order to overcome this difficulty it is advisable that the leader or leaders in charge of the playground should have some other appropriate appointment to occupy most of their time during the close season and so enable them to earn the necessary salary to make the job reasonably attractive. What such other occupation could be would depend partly on the leaders' capabilities and partly on what the city can offer in the way of part-time social service employment. The type of work that would appear to be most suitable in combination with adventure playground leadership would be something in the field of youth service or education. It might well go with the assistant leadership of a large youth club or some supervisory post in the school meal or the educational welfare services or even night school instruction. This is a matter to which careful consideration must be given if this type of work is ever to become an accepted profession and to spread throughout the larger towns and cities of the country.

3. *Controlling Committees.* While a local committee composed of social workers and other interested and influential people is very necessary for much of the administration of an adventure playground it has certain obvious weaknesses. In particular it lacks prestige and financial support and finds itself ineffective when obliged to negotiate with powerful corporation departments in such matters as acquiring fresh land or meeting the requirements of the town planners and architects. It is no insult to the members of the Pitt Street or the Youth Organisations Committees, the joint sponsors of the playground, to say that they lacked the full support necessary for carrying out a really first-class job of work. Too often money was lacking to purchase equipment *at the critical moment when it was urgently required* and there was never sufficient financial backing to assure a potential leader that the post had any prospect of reasonable security. The playground tended to live from hand to mouth and this resulted in little or no planning for the future. The whole enterprise had such a temporary appearance and such nebulous backing that it could never hope to be an attractive proposition to any well-qualified group worker.

The whole future of the playground movement in Liverpool and in other cities is very much in the balance. Not enough people believe in the value of the work, too little is known about its techniques and too few ordinary citizens are prepared to press for their development and extension. Public spirited individuals or little groups of local enthusiasts cannot hope to find their way through the complex tangle of administrative machinery, let alone raise the money, to carry on this vitally important work. Only a central committee, backed by the full support of the City Council, and representing both the voluntary and statutory organisations in equal partnership, can hope to carry through a programme which could cope with the many problems involved. What the city really needs is a Playground Adviser to act as secretary of such a joint-committee, whose job would be to supervise the work of existing playgrounds, to stimulate local support, train fresh workers and be responsible for pioneering new projects. Such a scheme demands firm financial backing. That backing only comes from belief in the value of the project. It is in the hope that the story of one pioneer venture will help to stir public imagination and stimulate community action that this report has been written and circulated.

APPENDIX

A Note on Finance

It is difficult to estimate the exact cost of running the playground for two reasons. First, the adventure section expenditure was incorporated in the yearly accounts which covered all sections of the playground, although in fact it comprised about 80 per cent of the entire outlay. Secondly, a great many gifts were received either in kind or in service and this included not only equipment and materials donated by city business houses but also maintenance of the site, repair of netting, etc. which the Liverpool Education Committee carried out free of charge. The Local Authority moreover bore the entire cost of insurance coverage and permitted the Pitt Street Committee to occupy the site free of rent and rates.

The National Playing Fields Association made an annual grant of £400 for two years towards the cost of the leader's salary. A further £545 was received from the Liverpool Youth Organisations Committee's Central Playground Fund while a gift of £200 towards the cost of laying on water and erecting a hut came through the Liverpool Council of Social Service. Without these substantial financial contributions it would have been quite impossible to have launched such an ambitious project.

The total expenditure during the two years that a full-time leader was in charge was £1,570. Since this sum included certain capital and non-recurrent expenditure on such things as fencing, drains, erection of hut, etc. it would probably be fair to estimate that, following the initial outlay, the playground could run on an annual income of about £700 a year. This would be divisible into an allocation of £400 to the salary of a leader, and about £150 per annum to purchase of tools, equipment, sand, etc. and a similar amount to repairs and renewals to existing fittings.

www.ingramcontent.com/pod-product-compliance
Ingram Content Group UK Ltd.
Pitfield, Milton Keynes, MK11 3LW, UK
UKHW021325180426
11947UKWH00017B/1450